POEMS

FROM OUR

YOUNG

The Literary Journey of Sierra Leone's
New Century Poets

Jermaine Carew - Esmeralda Simpson
Keira Forde - Mariam Mansaray

Edited by Winston Forde

The Authors

Jermaine Nnamdi Carew

Born in the United Kingdom and raised in Freetown, Sierra Leone, Jermaine Nnamdi Carew realised his literary potential early after hours of storytelling to his younger brother, Amani. He authored two 2-storied novels titled Tiger Fist and the Golden Gloves of Heracles at fourteen. He continued his education in the United States after being forced to emigrate due to the Ebola crisis. He is an alumnus of Apex International School, OBHS, Dublin Coffman High School and Miami University, with a Bachelor of Science Degree in Kinesiology & Health, majoring in Public Health. He currently works as the LLCHC COVID Testing Coordinator.

Esmeralda Simpson

Esmeralda Simba Kuhl Simpson is an African European aged twenty-two who lives in Ghana. She grew up in Freetown, Sierra Leone attending the Apex International School where she developed her interest in writing. Over some years now she has written several poems whilst toying with the idea of writing her first Novel. Since arriving in Ghana to continue her schooling Simba has become a well known model and produced some compelling Art work. However her potential as a Writer has always been uppermost in her discussions with the Editor and she has reluctantly ventured into publishing her first book of poems. She hopes to continue writing poetry and will not stop until she eventually delivers her first Novel. She has constantly been encouraged by her family and close friends who are proud to be able to see Simba become a published Writer.

Keira Forde

Keira Forde was born and raised in York, England. She's had a love for literature ever since she started primary school. Aside from reading, Keira spends a lot of time rowing and spending huge amounts of money on books and food with her friends. She hopes to go to university and continue as an author. Her first novel is entitled At a Glance.

Mariam Mansaray

Mariam Fatima Kabiru Mansaray is a Sierra Leonean. She started writing as a little girl. She is an alumna of the Fourah Bay College, University of Sierra Leone, with a Bachelor of Arts Degree and is currently a Law Student. Over the years, she has written poems and short stories, even though most of her writings were never published. She however continued to write with the hope that one day she will be a published author. Writing for her is not only a way of showing one's creativity or imagination, but also considers it as therapeutic.

Poems from our Young

Dedication

To our future writers

Acknowledgements

This has been a labour of love…..

We thank our parents and teachers for their love and guidance in our education, also their faith in our abilities.

I thank Elsa Maria Lindqvist, Swedish co-Author with Meera Chakravorty, India of a Book of Poems entitled The Remnant Glow, for reviewing some of Simba's poems with helpful comments.

I also thank Anni Domingo, a celebrated actress on stage and television from Sierra Leone for her keen interest in our young Poets and her encouragement. She is a lecturer, director and MA graduate of Anglia Ruskin Creative Writing and has published poems and short stories. Her first Novel, The MAAFA Chain based on the story of the young Sarah Bonetta was shortlisted in the Lucy Cavendish College Fiction Prize winning Myriad Editions First Novel Competition and will be published in 2021.

Finally, we cannot thank Uncle Coolie aka Grandpa enough for helping us with our writing over the years and for being the architect of this Anthology.

About the Book

I have had to live up to the amazing names given to me by my parents and Godparents: *Winston* inspired me to join the Royal Air Force and engage in Politics as a local Councillor and to write; *Lemuel*, a diminutive of Samuel led me to lifelong service in the Church as a Chorister, Sunday School Teacher, PCC and Deanery Synod member. I welcome this latter opportunity to become involved with Poetry by encouraging our young writers to publish this Anthology in line with *Alfred Lord Tennyson,* my namesake.

Having published several Books and been involved with developing two Publishing Houses connected with Sierra Leone, I finally formed my own Literary Agency to enable me to continue to work with writers as an Editor and general facilitator. I enjoy nurturing young writers and after working closely with Jermaine Carew to publish his first two books and with Keira Forde, our granddaughter who recently released her first Novel, At a Glance, both as teenagers I am proud to have encouraged these four young Poets to keep on writing.   I believe they are now ready to show the World what they are capable of writing and wish them every success in future publications.

Winston Lemuel Tennyson Forde
http://winstonfordebooks.com

A brief Review by Anni Domingo

This anthology is innovative and comes at a time when we must all look to the young people for the kind of future we all have as we move through the very difficult time of COVID-19. The four writers have all found ways to link us to our pasts as well as our future. The poems are thoughtful and moving. it is good to see that the voice of our young people is going to be heard through this anthology

Contents

Poems from our Young

**The Historic Cotton Tree
Freetown, Sierra Leone**

JERMAINE CAREW

The Cotton Tree:
Root, Trunk and Leaves

The Root

Over two centuries and a half ago,
began the existence of the cotton tree.
A tree that is symbol to the land of the free,
founded by a people whose stories are untold,
drawn from places where their lives were sold.
Some descended from Igbo and are also of the Yoruba,
others were former slaves from England and America,
some were freed in Jamaica and Canada.
All came to this place called the mountain of lions,
by this tree a new home rooted in their promising Zion.

The Trunk

Before the tree could even experience its wonder,
the cold colonial grasp swooped over and yonder,
strung by the whip that cracked louder than thunder.
Cries of revolt break asunder,
lines run across along the tree bark,
keep the freed slaves and the natives separate!
Make one group act like us and keep the others
  desperate!
But how do you fight against guns and the English
  Bible,
learn their ways and reclaim your country's title?
Today the tree up to the trunk is protected by a fence,
to prevent strangers from disturbing our
  Independence,

The Leaves

As the coloniser goes back to his home over seas,
the leaves bloom green as people shout with glee.
Then the storms of corruption, war and greed,
blow a few leaves off the tree.
But the tree stands tall, helpful if it may,
the wind of hope would carry the leaves back someday.

Congo Market

Several stalls stand, built from wooden poles, covered
  roof toppings and umbrellas,
Several people filling the streets no matter the
  changing weathers,
cars oddly parked to avoid the crowded center.
One can hear the millions of bargains,
deals to sell the many fruits and franchise amidst the
  verbal jargons.

The language of the trade is not taught but learned,
it takes a few trips of venture with money earned.
What price can I get if I walked further down
and come across better looking products found?
That is the challenge of "following the market,"
whether cold water, mangoes, shoes, or a jacket.
If you want to buy something within a time bracelet,
you will talk to the seller long before you bury the
  hatchet.

The Dark Continent

The Dark Continent? What does that mean?
By what right do you call my continent when only our
    problems are seen?
Why do you pursue our perverse unfortunate events,
calling it, irredeemable?
Yet you have eaten our finest food and enjoyed our
    finest waters, calling it, unbelievable?
I am in confusion.

I will not hide it, all fifty four of us have
overlapping problems beyond our control,
poverty, drought, desertification, hunger all take their toll.
Over fifty plus years of freedom, we have continuously
shot ourselves in the foot,
corruption, wars, Boko Haram, land disputes,
tribalism are stains to our root.
We even partook in slavery, the ultimate sin,
divided by tribe, not seeing each other as kin.
Now we drown in our own delusion.

But the blame does not fall on only us,
we are just bullets from the gun of heavy costs,
like bullets we are blamed for our country's hopes
and dreams lost.
And they always forget about the trigger, the gun's tool
    to combust, to carry out the execution.

You know what is coming next,
but I would not raise the same old arguments

from the old texts.
Slavery, manipulation, colonialism, christian missionaries?
No, I am looking at the now and the next.
The negative news reporting, proxy wars, trade inequity,
Us versus Them, and continuous pretentious ignorance.

Why do you call my home, the Dark Continent?
Did none of your continents suffer in their own early
    stages?
Bubonic Plague, Civil Wars, Revolutions, Religious
    Discrepancies and other humans in cages?
When some of us get hit with an epidemic,
You resort to jokes and fear.

When one happens to you now,
you suddenly cry our tears.
When you visit, you are treated like guests and given
    our best,
when we visit, we are forced to conform to a nationality
    test.
There's more to say but I will stop here to avoid
    exclusion.

For time to come, we will always shift the blame,
it only stops when we start to claim,
we all have created this beast of no nation.
That still lurks during our celebration,
Would we all be alive to truly witness this change?
I do not know, and that is my conclusion.

Family; A Foreign Foundation

Whether we live together or separate continents apart,
everyone have their relation linked by blood or through the
  heart,
a bond cannot be worn out over the ocean.
Resisting the epidemics and pandemics of time,
effective only if contact is in motion.
Faith in others can elevate one from despair,
agape love and wisdom can topple down one's societal
  fear.
My gratitude for my family cannot be measured by a seer,
Invictus with family support can force courage to appear.
Love your fathers and mothers to climb the happiness
  stairs,
you don't have to be a foreigner to buy into this idea.

Tiger In Human Form

Kings do not all walk with followers nor a crown.
Be it the densest forest or the largest town,
I tread with authority that others are scared to follow,
they look on in envy, claiming my heart was hollow.
If a lion were here in all his pride,
you would praise his mane and go to his side,
this loudmouth you call 'King of Beast,'
I can never find a trail of him in the East.
If we were to ever fight,
I would teach him what is bark from bite.
I am not a monster,
Yet you track me down like a hunter.
If I walk alone, you call me lonely,
If I walk in a crowd, you call me your homie.
I am still friendly and I enjoy lots of carnivals,
I wish we could all live in peace as all animals.
If you all love this poem, then at the very least,
Go to Amazon.co.uk or .com and buy my book,
Tiger Fist...By Nnamdi Carew.

To The Good Apples

This query is not for the accused,
nor the ones who beat civilians and abuse.
Those individuals need not be named,
for their actions were already videotaped and more
mention would only increase their fame.
They are the bad apples that are to blame.

This query, however, is for the rest of the barrel,
the good apples who work with the bad to help those in
    peril,
Who demand respect when organisational problems are
    reported by guys like Darrell.
Who lay down their lives everyday,
who are called to serve from June to May.

I know you feel that the coverage of you is unfair,
but please bear with my civilian query if you care.
One similarity I believe that we both share,
is that we want to be acknowledged and praised for our
    humanity instead of fear.
I argue that you are most protected in society under law,
that any assault against you would be criminal with no
    context line to draw.

In court, your presence is of an authority without flaw,
you are seen as the guardian of the community,
who stops folks that see chaos as an opportunity.
I argue that you knew the bad apples' ploy,
but you either stay away or watch them destroy.
You dislike generalisations yet your tactics are the same
    when deployed,
your fraternal camaraderie can have a few flaws that
    contribute to the endless brutal void.

Nuance is the bridge of different thoughts,
I know I have not walked in your shoes full of cuts,
I know you fear for your life constantly on duty,
But not all thugs wear a hoodie,
Your career is to protect and not make me fear of being
    dead,
You are supposed to call those apples out when they
    behave like Judge Dredd,

Rank and hierarchy mean nothing to a civilian life,
when a knee on the neck is enough to end a constant
    strife.
Why is it serene without any justice?
Why does my look invite violence to you and not
    peace?
History marks no space for the silent good,
ask anyone in any of the neighbourhoods.

I implore you to hold your comrades when they are
    irresponsible,
we all want to feel safe around the big, strong constable.
You are not the true villain, but neither the true hero,
progress does not move forward if your actions remain
    zero.

To the good apples that look at me, I plead that you
    keep trying,
do not over consume what the system is lying.
You live two lives, there is no need to choose one.
Remember which side you are on at the barrel of a gun.
Hopefully, in the near future, if there is a hint or clue,
we would not associate beating and killing with being
    black and blue.

ESMERALDA SIMPSON

Liquid Lover

Can you be my rain?
The bringer of life,
the gentle lover that flows across my skin,
bringing a chill to the heat,
the one that brings me peace,
that makes me safe and complete.

Can you be my rain?
The one whose rhythm appeases my demons,
the lover whose touch makes me hum in delight,
that makes my world blaze in colours, even at night.

Can you be my rain,
the rain to my storm?

Cord of Panic

Thought I was getting better,
more resilient,
just a little bit stronger,
yet just words can crack.
It kills to know nothing has changed,
the smiles won't cover up no more,
as every thought yell it's your fault.
The helpless demon screams from its vaults.
A voice flickers with an apology for never being
enough,
they clash with a force that shakes deep,
every core trembles and twists till breathing fail to
stay or leave, fear chokes and suffocates,
whilst tears pour down redden cheeks.
The saltiness is a bitter reminder of a weakness so
vast,
I'm reminded of the brokenness that's covered with a
façade of external happiness,
used to mask all the ugliness inside.
The guilt and shame crashes and burns every nerve,
yet hope is what keeps me alive,
hope that one day things will be different.
Hope is what pulls me slowly back from the recess of
my demons and into light that could be my future.

Scaredy Cat

Fear! Fear! Fear! Fear! Fear!
So cruel.
Why won't you leave me alone?
Always afraid,
always in despair,
always wondering,
when is it going to disappear?
Who really cares?
Whose really there?
Tears try to shoe the pain,
try to betray me and show the hurt,
its fight or flight all within.
Trying to win a war that knows no defeat,
nor end for the weak.
I can barely contain it,
it's emotional havoc.

Dark smiles

I die slowly inside,
from pains that are easy to hide,
and with a smile I wonder why?
I act strong in front of their eyes,
and so strong in front of their eyes,
and so weak alone in the dark,
where tears escape with a heart felt goodbye,
in sync with my muffled cries.
As memories so torturous start to fly by,
through a mind beaten and scared,
and praying for release.
Until finally kissed with a blissful sleep,
only to wake and realise the circle is still on repeat.

Senses Overload

Take me somewhere deep,
where my senses and mind sleep,
where my thoughts are cleansed, and my body is free,
where my illusions are made into dream,
where my heart's desires feel complete.
For under the sea,
as silence makes it easier to breathe,
as waves crash against my skin,
I float on a world only I can see.
Why should I leave?
'Cause though I'm lost,
I finally feel free.

Breaking Free

You were my King
I was your Queen
Till you left me to chase other things
For a minute I forgot the strength I had within
You broke me
Crippled me till I was bleeding and begging on my
knees
For forgiveness and mercy, I didn't need
But now I'm back to my senses and stronger than I've
ever been
Reclaiming my throne, ruling my kingdom on my
own
Building a fortress powerful no intruder dare evade
For this is where I will stay
Invisible
No one will hurt me ever again

Wishful thinking

I wish I was pretty
Then I wouldn't be so lonely
Yet lately
Ive found it's more about personality
So I wish I wasn't so broken
But then I'm doing too much wishing
And quite honestly it's exhausting
Trying to pull it all together
But I still cant help but wish I was stronger
To be able to do better
Yet how many wishes can one make till
They can't wish any longer?

Calm

I look around and ask myself what is it that I want
But only found the answer when I closed my eyes and
  took a breath
Fame, money, power, love nothing compared to that
single moment
When my lungs filled with fresh cool air
Whilst taking away all the stress
The peace as my closed eyes silence my mind
That right there was the answer I sought
That feeling of enlightened calmness
Yesterday became fond memories rather than burdens
Tomorrow became obsolete
And the present, well it was all that mattered

Pointless expression

I open my mouth to speak
But it closes 'cause I think what's the point?
It doesn't matter what I say or think
People's perception would never change
It's just a waste of breath
Pointless energy
Trying to express how your actions affected me
So I don't react
'Cause what's the point?
I simply acknowledge it and move on.

Pain

I wish I could tell you what's in my heart
The words, they pause
Cuz trust is lost
They pile up inside
Buried under pretence
I'm scared that's what I want to shout
I'm so afraid
I doubt anyone cares
I pray to have faith
To be strong and deal with it
But weakness creeps in like a slithering snake
It sucks the strength and leaves me broken,
weak and in pain
In doubt and insane
My eyes gorge up tears
Panic builds up
I'm losing time
But there's so much fear
Getting closer to the end
Losing myself
Losing my mind
Feeling sorry for all that's lost
It's my fault
I'm sorry
It's my fault
I'm not brave enough
It's my fault
Maybe it isn't too late to change
It's my choice.

Vain Reflection

I look in the mirror and try to find what you see in me
Try to see all the wonders that you proclaim is within
But it doesn't matter if it's a gaze or a prolonging stare
All I see is flaws overbearing in everything
Eyes hollowed and lost to pain
Shadow and baggage betrays the mental stability that
    pretence portray
Lips cracked and dried up, in need of nourishment
and faded behind a smile that covers the fact
What beauty do you speak of?
To what shows evidence of your truth
Or are your words a flattering emptiness
To fulfil what you wish to gain
Perhaps your words speak in favour of my character
Yet even that is rather misleading
For how can you judge something you haven't studied
Something in which you show no interest?
I'd skip the lies and spew the horrid truth
So at least I can stop searching in vain.

Double Standards

You say I'm perfect
You say I'm great
You say I'm beautiful in every way
Why does it all sound fake?
Your touch
Your smile
So loving
So kind
You treat me like a queen that I can't deny
You say the right things all the time
So easy so smooth, I'm sure it's all lies
But maybe it's true
That you mean it when you kiss my lips and say
I love you too
I'm sorry to say
Letting you in isn't worth the pain
If it did turn out to be all a game.

Pure Intentions

I'm falling in love with the music that is you
A lullaby so pure
Every tone timed to the melody of my soul
It seeps deep
And calms a restless heart that yearns for a love that
doesn't end in pain
A song that proves that your love will give me all the
happiness I can gain
That won't end in vain
Yes, I'm falling in love with the music that is you
The one only you can play
The one that lights up my day
Changing me for the better in every way.

Misunderstood

I'm scared of the way you make me feel
It's new, it's foreign
And scary too
The problem is it feels good
I'm afraid to lose it
I'm afraid to keep it
I'm afraid it won't matter cause you will still hurt me
and leave
And nothing will be the same
You won't care it hurts
You won't think of the pain you've caused
You will walk out
And I won't be the same.

Taken For Granted

It happened
It finally did
I was happy
I was floating
It seemed surreal
Much more a dream
Past the realm of reality
I wondered, was it all an illusion
Made by a tired mind
Was the adrenaline nothing but a façade?
No I felt the pounding of my heart
No more a ghost in my chest
But I cant help but think if I imagined it all
Was I confused?
Blinded to the truth
Craving that's kinda high
That's why you became the drug that took over my
life
Now I'm an addict with no turning back.

Unstable

Can't breathe
Can't move
So paralysed my mind's gone
Want to disappear
Want to hide
Can't take this pressure
Can't take these lies
Can't take the reality
It's so sad
I'm broken
Long gone
Can't find where to be saved
Can't take any voices
Can't take any pain
So loud, I'm about to explode
So full there's nowhere to go
Crushed hopes
Crushed dreams
Maybe sleep will bring me peace.

Advantages

I let you in
You don't see how that causes me pain
To have someone know me
Having someone close
Being vulnerable
It's a scary thing
So I prefer to stay by myself
It's easier, less complicated
I'm safe and protected
In control
But with you
My brokenness is in full view
You see the flaws
You gain the power to destroy
And it hurts that I know you will
It's nothing new.

Lost Love

When you met me,
I have to admit,
my heart wasn't in the right place.
My soul had already gone into protective mode,
blocking out anything that could have brought back
the pain from before.
Words, promises, nothing you said,
would register in my head,
'cause those were the ones that left me broken - dead.

But then again, I must admit,
that even if it was for a little bit,
you showed my heart the direction to the right place.
But you had already moved on,
I guess I realised it too late.

Empty Host

She was trapped, and confused,
lost in a world she didn't choose.
Lesser than a ghost,
drifting through an empty host,
trying to find what matters most.

Betrayals And Truths

In a world of lies and hidden truths,
where words are spoken in codes and nothing said is true,
with evil hearts,
and backstabbing minds,
fake love and fake smiles,
please remember to think twice,
'cause nothing fragile or naïve can survive.

Cursed

I don't want to be saved,
I'm not waiting on a knight with shining armour to
recuse me from my distress.
For I bask in the emptiness,
it's a self-inflicted punishment,
the emotional tumour being my way of rectifying all
the wrongs I've caused.
to take responsibility for the damage I've done.
It's the same as the blade crossing your veins,
or the alcohol that drowns your lungs,
only mine is the ache in my heart, as it squeezes so
tight my lungs can't expand.
It's an addiction far more perverse than nicotine,
the pushing away any happiness and causing the pain,
it's something I need to feel.
it's payment,
it's judgement.
Don't try to understand or tell me different!
You'd never understand and I never want you to,
It's not a competition!
Don't tell me yours is worse than mine,
maybe it is, maybe I'm just weaker,
Am allowed to be.
And if you have a problem then be my guest and walk
   away,

like the rest of many,
I advise you to not even waste your time,
just walk away, leave.
I'm done with feeling,
I'm done believing,
I'm done.
Nothing to hold me but my pain,
it fills me till I can't breathe,
and I smile 'cause at least it's something that always
stays the same.

Survival

I've learnt to hide the pain,
so many words can't say out loud 'cause words can't
  even explain.
So, I stuck my head in the clouds,
to forget every broken promise that's stained in my
  brain,
and every memory that flows through my veins.
Oh, how you make me happy, only to leave me in
  disdain,
they say you got to be strong though,
you've got to hold on.
Figure it out and prove them they're wrong,
make them wish they had never left you alone,
make them regret every minute they're gone.
I wish it was as easy as it sounds,
so, I can accomplish it right here and now.
But honestly without you I'm feeling more lost than
  found,
don't get me wrong, I'm slowly turning my frown
  upside down.

Cheated Heart

Why did you cheat?
I loved you so much,
I give you so much,
I stood by your side,
I give you my heart.
Our love was beautiful, it was art.

Why did you cheat?
Wasn't I enough?
Weren't we happy?
What was it you wanted that you risked every I love you's.
every memory we ever created.

Why did you cheat?
Did you not think it would hurt me?
Was it all a game?
You said you would marry me,
what changed?

I even forgave you once,
sacrificed all that I was to make us work.
opened up to all your flaws and loved every one.
At the end what hurts the most,
is not that you played me for a fool,
took me for granted and left me feeling lost and confused.
No!
What hurts is that I have to give you up,
when out of everything, you were what I most wanted.

Rania

Rania,
The sound of your name brings back memories,
of a time when happiness was on my mind.
But what you didn't see,
was all the pain that was in me.
You see you made me smile when my world was down,
you made me laugh when you were around,
I don't think you realised how hard that was to do,
how special you are,
That's true!
When we talked, you never failed to make me feel
    loved,
we shared a bond even though we aren't related, yet you
    treated me like we were sisters from the same blood.
"Big sister" you once said,
I think that the first time I've ever felt proud of myself.
I remember every detail about you,
favourite things, and even ones that irritated me too.
I remember how I admired how happy you were,
I swear that it was contagious too.
But now I'm gone,
and life has to go on,
yet your name remains in my heart,
'cause it took place of all the sadness that once tore me
    apart,
To be honest I don't know whether to smile or cry,
when I remember who you are.
my sister, my friend, the person who always made me
    laugh and coloured my life.

Frozen

Stuck between playing the victim or villain.
Hearts torn,
Can't tell between what's right, and what's wrong.
So many it's running through,
A mind disconnected from body and soul.
With a past passing through too hard to behold,
where forgetting is harder than I've been told.

Yeah times have changed,
evolving as I grow old.
I'm trying to make sense of the lessons taught,
aiding me along the path as while I find the right road.
Can't help but be confused,
what am I to do?

Society

The world wants me to be happy.
It wants me to help spread all the love,
to keep me and others around smiling,
the laughter rolling.

I was brought here to help,
to encourage,
to guide those to the light that the world had shown me,
the bliss of joy that was bestowed to me.

However, society had other intentions.
They needed me to be selfish,
they needed me to be mean,
told me I had to learn how to play the game.

Kindness is taken for granted,
makes you weak.
You have to be selfish if survival is what you wish.

Young Survival

Growing up in the street,
had you doing things to survive,
that killed your body and soul inside,
turned your eyes to a world you didn't want to see,
turned you slowly insane.

Instead of shutting down and cry,
your pain turned into an anger you couldn't deny,
with no one to protect and save you from that path.
You became someone even you couldn't recognise.
Though regret you couldn't deny,
Circumstances left a mark too deep to change your mind.

So, you grew bitter,
closed off,
always looking over your shoulders.
For in the end, it's only you that's there to pull
yourself together.

Sweet Me

I was born with a rare heartbeat,
that controls the way I move my feet,
that makes me feel unique,
and very special indeed.

I may have many flaws,
but one thing is sure,
there's no one like me.

I will make you laugh,
show you the time of your life,
and you won't mind how creepy and weird I'm like.

I might even teach you some new stuffs,
open your eyes to a whole new world,
and who knows you might fall in love.

Perfection

Perfection.
The irony is it leads to destruction.
Why?
Because it's nothing but mere illusions,
filled with individuals fighting due to different
  expectations.
Trying to gain a world with no bad intentions,
but forgetting that without imperfections,
the perfections would lose their attraction.

Just a simple observation.

Living

Life is nothing but a pain,
all that matters is what you gain,
though all the hurt shall remain,
please let the love stay the same.
I wanted to write this poem,
I know the journey is long,
but I pray you take your prayers along.

It's time to live,
make peace with who your inside,
embrace the big bright world outside.

Now I know how scary it is out there,
Oh, I've felt every single doubt and fear.
Because the world is made to break your soul,
make you feel less whole.
Just remember to breathe,
hold your heart close to your chest,
and think how special you are to be chosen,
to be brought to this earth.

Esmeralda Simpson

When The Rain Pours

And the coldness sweeps into my bones
Only thoughts of you slither into my mind
To pull you close
Your warmth holding me
Where I feel safe and peaceful
The rhythm of your heartbeat
The tapering sounds of rain drops
The cool air
And then reality crashes in
And I realise you are no more there
So I lay alone
In an empty bed, missing your touch
As tears escape
Too bad we've said good bye
Yet when rain pours,
You are where my thoughts run too.

Heartbreak

My heart is sad, it aches of you.
The pain tightens my chest and steals my breath.
My mind says I hate you but my heart still
won't stop missing you.
Tears turn to sob at memories that once was and
for the promise of a future that's now lost.
I'm as a walking wound - scabs peeling off whenever
I'm trigged into remembering you.
Some days I feel the battle has been won,
then I'm soon reminded that the war is far from done.
Patiently waiting when I will wake and my soul
won't choose you as the one.
When I won't be tortured every time I think, or see you.
Just your name causes me to hurt, why am I surprised?
I broke down my walls for you, guess it wasn't
enough, I'm forced to be cold and selfish to survive this.

My mind is telling me I hate you,
that you're not good for me.
My heart is telling I can't be without you, that we're
meant to be, my body is telling me I need you,
it craves your touch.
Is this love?
My confusion of a heartbreak I hope won't leave me
more damaged than I already am.

My Random Thoughts

It's hard to accept the truth when we so desperately
want it to be another way
We hurt ourselves by believing in change and having
faith
At times logic is the only light to guide us from
certain heartbreaks
Yet we ignore our thoughts
The warning flashing all around us
Hoping,
Grasping at anything that could prove us wrong
Yearning for things that we should know better of
But there's certain closure that stems from acceptance
When you are backed into the corner to face the
negatives that you've sought to avoid
When the fight dies out and the hope completely
diminishes
It's a numbing calmness
The what-if's, disappear
Knowing you did all you could
That you don't have to second guess whether there's
still something you could have done
That is the peace.

———————————————

Hold me Please
And never let me go
But caution
I'm gonna put up a fight
I'm gonna scream
I'm gonna bite
I'm gonna push
Im gonna be so difficult
Holding on is gonna be harder than letting go

—————————

I wished my soul would heal
I didn't mean to get it so broken
But the world is cruel
My memories attempt to grasp when I didn't believe
that to be true
To try and remember when innocence bloomed
But if I had ever been a child
Would I have been the woman I am now?
Fighting, surviving, loving and kind
Would I be proud of the reflection in the mirror?
At least now,
my suffering comes with dignity
I'm nothing yet proud

—————————

I wish I could draw, paint,
I wish I could have a talent that I could express all
these emotions churning inside of me
All the beauty that steals my breath away
All the darkness that caves in my system
I wish I could show the world everything I see
Why I stop to stare at the sunset
Why the night sky makes me smile
Why the full moon makes me gasp
I feel incredibly full with all these feelings
So much
So much
I wish I was a singer
To breathe into you, the feelings I get watching the
birds fly in the blazing sky
The colours that hug me when I stroll through the
dawn
Life, I'm in Love with it. I'm in love with the bad and
the good. Sights, sounds, smells, everything gives me
goosebumps.
The smell of trees, the wind blowing through my hair,
the air flowing through my lungs. So sweet, so crisp I
could cry. Overwhelmed with tears of joy, of sorrow,
of bewilderment.
I could laugh, giggle, and smile at it all.
I would want to capture it, freeze every moment in
time.

———————————

Do you trust what you see
or is it filled with deceit?
Are the lies the truth you must believe?
Yet here I stand with all my honesty
speaking truths when words around me twirl with
lies.,
where deciphering between the two takes up too
much energy.
I'm left with no choice but isolation,
staying away from what I can't control.
However it leaves me lonely in my soul,
saddened,
clouding my vision, blinded with judgement and
distrust.
How can happiness be filled when the people we love
betray us?
How can we be content always second guessing those
we love?
Picking, choosing, games of who could care less more
whilst pleading to connect with an individual,
as is our basic instinct.
Thinking strength breeds from being hard
in mind and in heart,
when does it become enough, or are you really
stronger with impenetrable walls

———————————

You know those moments
When you feel your very being breaking into tiny
little pieces
And you just can't breathe
'Cause everything hits you all at once
All those thoughts and emotions you've managed to
keep locked up
All those feelings you've thought had been done and
through with
Escaping as you shatter apart
Those are moments where the world seems devoid of
love
No colours, no hope
All you wanna do is curl up in a ball and just not
exist.
You can't even run, 'cause the battle is all inside of
you
And even your head is a scary place
You can't let it show though
In those moments
All you can do is power through
Smile, laugh, hold your head up high
And go about your day as if you didn't just die a little
more inside

____

My emotions churn in my head
Feeling tired
Feeling scared
Feeling lost, feeling confused
Why is it my heart and head are always divided in
two
All the answers swirl right in front me yet so far out
of reach
Shackled by pain and misery
my strength dwindles more everyday
Thinking how much more can one take

———————————

I see you
I see all the bad in you
I see all the demons you battle
I see the blackness clinging to your soul
I see you fight to be better everyday
I watch you as you shrink away
Scared that others would see
Terrified they'd pull away
What a shame
'Cause I think you're awesome no matter your pain
A noble warrior
A fighter
Someone to admire

———————————

I have this taste in my mouth
This lingering feeling
That reminds me of star burst and menthols
That takes my mind eye on a trip
Where memories flood and drown my thoughts
This taste, so subtle, so soft, in every corner I twist
my tongue
I can't stop tasting, deciphering it's origins
A moment that takes my senses to you
It's a part of me
Something that caves in my energy

———————————

I'm at a lack of words
As 3am dawns and sleep still evade my tired eyes
My senses are overwhelmed by the winds whistling
through my window sill
Caressing across my skin ever so gently
Blowing cool breeze from the tip of my nose, softly
across my bosom and down my finger tips
Traveling with scents that take my thoughts on a trip
As I lay in a bed that hugs me snuggly
Even the mosquitoes buzzing busily about can't take
away the magic of the moment
I'm utterly bewitched
Entranced by its Beauty in an ugly time
My soul at such peace
My senses set ablaze
I want nothing more than to bottle it up so that I can
always have it
But at last, I shall lay by my window letting the wind
take my worries away

———————————

Emotions are a funny thing
They creep inside you
Uncontrollable, unsupervised
Unexpected, untimely
It takes hold and refuses to let go
Grips you tightly
And leaves you to mend the falling pieces that break
apart
It won't leave till it's ready
Taking host in a body unwillingly
Unwelcome, unwanted

Uncaring, unsettled
Shifting, affecting everything without cause
It's a constant fight, as mind tries to reason with what
is right

———————-

Your hugs are laced with hurt
your kisses sting my lips with pain .
Yet I crave the comfort only you can provide.
Even though it's the very thing killing me inside.
Why I can't let you go I will never know
So I keep on breaking apart to keep you close
Maybe one day it will be easier to let you go
But for now I will wait till I'm numb to my core

———————

Take a deep breath
Forget about the headache
Just close your eyes and rest
Let the tears slip past
The sadness heavy on your chest
Sobbing quietly in dark
There's no peace in your thoughts

Realising the mess you've made
Falling for the wrong one
Now unable to move on
Stuck in circle
Unhappy as they come
What I wouldn't give for you to do the right thing
Maybe we weren't meant to be
So why cant I leave?

Stuck in a circle you see
Crying out from the hurt
I lost count how many times Iv'e let it go
Mending the heart you broke

Its circle you see
Maybe we weren't meant to be
But my stubborn heart won't give up hope
Can't wait for the day it decides not to love you anymore
Hopefully this torture won't last

It's a circle you see
It hurts more how the affection turns sour
Slowly killing the butterflies

Pretty soon I wont love you and I can be happy again.

When I heard that Mr. Winston had tested positive for the Corona Virus and been Hospitalised, I was moved to write this:

Corona

I'm not the only one to see
How different the world has come to be
Reality has morphed into a nightmare
filling the masses with fear,
The poor are dying, suffering the most
The ignorant plough through the streets without remorse
Others lay caged in what they once called home
The infected lay desolate in hospital beds praying for
    miracles
The world is bleeding, people cry out for hope,
Families can't say goodbye to their dead anymore
My heart aches for those with no where to go
My chest gets heavy at how low the mortality rate has
    fallen
Once an innocent sneeze it's now a sudden cause of panic
Even our leaders have left us to fend for ourselves in
    this pandemic
I bow my head, pray to my God
guide and protect me
For this is a future unstable and unpromised
Give me strength to survive
Yet even I aren't immune to the mental and emotional
    constraints
My sobs are all there is to console me when my mind
    caves and all gets dark
Suddenly priorities shift
What was once of importance no longer catches your
    mind
How could it when all you think is how to survive?

Losing trust in the very system that was placed to
  protect us
The Year 2020 made history
When The Corona humbled the globe

57

KEIRA FORDE

Dear World

Dear old family,
You give me strength,
When life makes no sense,
You make me laugh,
You make me cry,
You make me feel like,
I'm as tall as the sky.

I'm forever grateful.

Dear old friends,
Day after day,
You put a smile on my face,
Moving my heart,
Like a poltergeist,
When life presents no grace.

I'm forever grateful.

Dear old society,
You extirpate my strength,
Day after day after day,
The torment,
Has no relent.
When will you stop?
The massacre of egos,
Slaughtering and torturing,
Weakening at the knees,
Stings as strong as bumble bees.

For this I'm forever hateful.

The people closest to you,
Provide you with the strength,
It's the ones who don't know you,
Who cause the offence.

What can I say?
This is how its meant to be,
As society would say,
Veni vidi vici.

Keira Forde

Cloud Nine

A gleam of opal and amber,
Stretched across the sky.
Families gather around the bonfire,
Every eye is dry.

Humans are so full of glee,
Dancing between buttercups,
Undulating on the sea.

If every person loves to do so,
What is wrong with me?

Why don't I glide around the flowerbeds,
Sing a swaying song?
Why can't I stretch a smile,
Across these lips so drawn and long?

They love to laugh and dance and play,
To entertain for days and days,
To be merry and happy,
To savour the day.

Maybe another time,
I tell myself,
I'll dance just like everyone else.
I'll be happy,
I'll be free,
Maybe the pure guilt,
Will stop eating at me.

Nature

This is for the people
For the breaking
The crying
The ones who feel like dying.
The happy ones
The angry ones
The dancing ones
The prancing ones
The ones who feel like stars
For the girls
The boys
Those who don't know what they are.
This is for the animals
From tiny to enormous
Those who are furry
Those who are scary.
So many different characters
Like the incandescent stars
We lay below.
Us creatures seem to make others fall
Instead of helping them grow.
Let's be kind
Use our minds
To sprout the growth of love.
What good is hate
In a world so beautifully innate
That anything goes.

A Broken Artefact

I am an artefact.
My body is not to be marvelled upon
Or respected in any kind.
It is to be speculated upon
As if I have no conscious mind.
Each inch of skin
Boasting a vibrant melanin
Expose a certain vulnerability
That I struggle to keep within.
I am an artefact
That no one holds to their heart
I am but a stuffed monkey
Scarce of God's sacred art.

Bandwagon

Jump on the bandwagon,
Don't be left behind!
Run dear friend,
Or be hung out to dry.

The bandwagon is such a beautiful place,
Painted with rainbows,
In all its glorious grace.

Everybody loves the bandwagon,
Nobody can resist!

Come on,
Jump on!

Don't be ridiculous.

One time,
Just once,
I missed the bandwagon,
It passed me like an almighty dragon,
I felt the breeze on my face,
As I waved goodbye to the human race.

And for a while no one came back for me,
The bandwagon was the centre of their life.
Like a daisy in the sun,
It helped them to thrive,
in a world that wants to see you die.

At last the bandwagon came back for me,
A man held out his hand.

I took graciously,
And never turned back around.

Now dear friend,
Now do you see,
Why the most important thing,
Is for you to follow me?
Please hop on,
Don't let them know you're different,
Or get carried away in the vicious torrent.

The torrent of society,
That wants to see people like you and me,
Thrown to our deaths,
For our natural dubiety.

So never question it,
Like I once did,
Don't let them know,
or suffer eternal hatred.

Playground

My heart is nothing but a ball of putty to you.
To be stretched
And thrown
And moulded
How you want it.

My brain is nothing but the control centre to you.
To be hardwired
And reprogrammed
To appreciate
Your twisted version of
Love.

My eyes are nothing but property to you.
To be plagued by
Dishonour and
Adultery
With no real proof.

My hair is nothing but a rope to you.
To be pulled
And broken
At every harsh
Tug.

My body is nothing but a playground to you.
To be enjoyed
And mistreated
Like the carelessness
Of youths.

My love is nothing but a lever to you.

A chain reaction
Of false promise
And affection
Leading to my heart.

You do not love me
So don't pretend
You just want a toy
So your boredom never
Ends.

Property

Please
Don't make this harder
Take your leather bound suitcase
Filled with the sad memories of being
A martyr to your love.
Take your old cashmere jumper
Smothered in the precious blood and tears
Of my own body.
Take that dirt cheap hair gel
Diaphanous enough to bind your wire-like hair
undetected
Not enough to coalesce our hearts.
Take that tessellated mini cooper
And drive down the old dirt road.
Do not turn back for a final look
A final glance
Into your murderous past.
This is pain
This is torture
This is a tremendous loss of time
But it's worth it
So I'll never be in as much despair
As the days where I was forced to call you
Mine.

Necessity

I don't need you.

You don't provide for me,
Like orcas need the sea.
You have never loved me,
Like how you would in my dream.

Your only concern,
Is the flesh on your bones,
The radiant blood,
That you boastfully claim as your own.

I don't need you.

The gleaming smile playing across your lips,
The golden sparkle in your very iris,
Cause a fluttering in my heart,
That makes me want you to never depart.

I don't need you.

Every night,
I lay there,
Mascara ridden face,
Wondering why the human race
Cares for others,
Who treat them like dirt,
Their hellos and goodbyes
Are distastefully curt,

I don't need you,
I don't need you,

I really don't.
I know that,
I always have,
Right from the start.
The only problem is,
Try telling that to my heart.

Greed

Steer clear of the urge,
Don't come close to the verge,
of a sensation you can't resist,
Or your mind will conjure to mist.

For it is a common event,
We humans cannot prevent,
The plate is woefully full,
Do not empty or befoul,
Your own stomach cannot digest,
The sheer juice of the biting zest.

So next time you indulge,
Your sheer greediness could divulge.

Be careful dear friend,
Or this pleasure could just come to an
End.

Give Me A Reason

Give me a reason to trust you,
Give me a reason to hold you,
Give me a reason to believe you,
So I know we'll make it through.

No words or art,
Could cover the casket of lies.
The catacomb of trust,
Laying beneath the broken skies.

I want a reason to trust you,
To hold you like my own.
A reason to believe that maybe your soul,
Is putrid just like mine,
Rotting under the pressure of society's crime.

But you give me no reason to trust you,
To hold you like my own.
To cherish and to treasure,
Like a seedling of Earth's home.
All you've given me is reasons,
To hide beneath the dirt.
To put my sacred life on halt,
In the fear that you'll get hurt.

Help me oh friend,
Or thats what I'd like to call you.
But how can I be like a mother to you?
Nourish you and care for you.
I guess I can't,
So this is how it will be,
A soft wave from the distance,
An adieu to thee.

Trigger

I remember the first time it was said to me
It slithered off his tongue
And pierced my ear drum
With it's r-shaped
Tail.

It chewed at my self esteem
And whirled through my mind
With disbelief.

The idea that it's just a word
Is nothing short of absurd.
It tells a story of struggle
And pain
And anguish
Of the thousands slain
By oppression and
Systematic slander.

Do not make light
Of a word made to discredit
The dark.
Not only does it damage my future
It damages my heart.

This word I'm thinking of is not
Tigger
Or vigor.
Nor is it
Digger
Viger
Rigger
Or snigger.

The word I'm thinking of
Which you take such delight in saying
Is much
much
Bigger.

Idle

Letting your guard down,
Could cost a life.

Being inattentive,
Will impale you like the knife,
I sharpened for your sacrifice.

Of all the mistakes made by a human,
Lazing around is by far the top reason,
For phenomenons way beyond our control,
Sparking the rise of the imminent death toll.

Do you want to witness the massacre
Of time?
The life draining out,
Bleeding from the mind.
No answer needed,
I know what you think.
So get up from your sofa,
And don't come close the brink.

Jettison

Like a hangnail
I'll be there for a while
Showing you
Reminding you
Of that one small error.

Don't be dim
Just tear me off
Relieve yourself from the terror.

It'll hurt like hell on Earth
But oh how you'll be glad you did it.

Go on
I know you want to.
Just tear
Or suffer eternal despair.

Two Doves

Of roses we'll hold
Under the late night's blue
And you'll tie our menet
Around my bruised neck.
An intertwine of fingers
A strum of the harp
To ignite a passion
That'll burn so sharp.

And when our love dries out
I'll cry by the arroyo
And clasp a claddagh between
My palms.
Our hearts will scream telepathic
Psalms
As I long for the warmth
Of your open arms.

Betrayal

Every secret I shared with you,
Every moment I lived with you,
Every breath I took for you,
Even when I envied doom,
All because I trusted you.

For months on end,
I've felt an inkling,
That maybe all the fun and drinking,
Was just your way of cutting through,
Of making me put all my trust in you.

But now I know why you rejoiced in my being,
Who knew such a human could have so little meaning.

Now every secret, every moment, every breath I gave
to you,
Feels like a blowing symphony,
A cynical blues.

Now dear friend,
You are more than just dead to me,
You're beyond non existent in my wildest dreams.

Destruction

New phone,
New home,
New life,
New loan,
All sacred things,
That we cherish from within.

One Earth,
A billion races,
One Home,
A thousand faces,
All sacred things,
That we spit on and we sin.

Now do you see where our priorities are wrong?
How the next trend or craze,
Captures us like the sun.
Our home is dying,
Day by day,
Rotting and weakening,
Slipping away.

Oh never mind,
Who cares anyway?
It's only tomorrow,
Live in today.

Empty

Caught in the throat,
Lost from my heart.
Swimming in my mind,
Dry in my eyes.

I need it,
I want it,
I crave it,
I'd save it.

I'm severely scarce of it.

As much as I want to scream and cry,
Yell from the highest point in the sky.
To feel something, anything,
Anything at all.

Besides,
Receiving the greatest pleasure,
Comes with the most fatal fall….

Escape

If life is like a box of chocolates,
Why must it taste so bitter?
If humans are so smart and powerful,
Why must we all litter?

All my life I've been fed a lie
Of omnipotence and clear blue skies.
But once reality hit me like a brick,
Life was no longer a huge green tick.

Ever since that dreaded day,
I've needed a distraction
To take me away.

Keira Forde

Give Me A Reason

Give me a reason to trust you,
Give me a reason to hold you,
Give me a reason to believe you,
So I know we'll make it through.

No words or art,
Could cover the casket of lies.
The catacomb of trust,
Laying beneath the broken skies.

I want a reason to trust you,
To hold you like my own.
A reason to believe that maybe your soul,
Is putrid just like mine,
Rotting under the pressure of societies crime.

But you give me no reason to trust you,
To hold you like my own.
To cherish and to treasure,
Like a seedling of Earth's home.
All you've given me are reasons,
To hide beneath the dirt.
To put my sacred life on halt,
In the fear that you'll get hurt.

Help me oh friend,
Or thats what I'd like to call you.
But how can I be like a mother to you?
Nourish you and care for you.
I guess I can't,
So this is how it will be,
A soft wave from the distance,

An adieu to thee.Just one grasp,
A little hook.
Nothing but a cup of tea
And a nice big book.

Lonely

The clock strikes three,
Finally we're free!
Sunshine and and lollies await us
By the sea.

Dancing across the open planes,
Singing songs for days and days.
Life just doesn't get better than this.

My happiness has become such a far miss.

Chatting and giggling,
They're full of glee,
But not one person has thought about me.

My feelings and emotions are all but futile,
To the people I call friends,
The ones who'd jump in front of a missile,
All for me.

Or so they say.

His smiles and laughs,
Cause a sickness in my tummy.
My head starts to whir,
My mouth feels all funny.

I'm surrounded by people who supposedly love me,
Who cherish me and care for me,
Like we are family.

But while we sit there,

Having so much fun,
I can't help but think of yesterday's conundrum.

The words he spoke,
Pierced me like bullets.
They angered my friends,
But only for a minute.

Don't over react,
That's what they always say.
Leave the problems behind,
And start a new day.

But they don't know,
What its like to be me.
To be ridiculed and laughed at,
For my skin and personality.

I'm surrounded by people who supposedly love me,
So why do I feel so incredibly lonely?

Isn't it funny,
How a dozen friends,
Will never support you,
When life feels at an end?

I'm surrounded by people who supposedly love me,
So why do I feel so incredibly lonely?

Silent Struggle

My house is empty,
Unfurnished and dull.
My garments are single toned,
bleak and dark in hue.
The field I once danced in,
sing a dark shade of blue.
When will someone start to see?

Life is evacuating
is evacuating,
Rushing and scrambling.
All has gone bleak,
All has gone black.

My heart is slowing,
The end is nigh.
I can feel it coming,
Oh how I wish I could cry.

For I have not perished in body or physique,
Only mind and spirit have left me so weak.

What Am I To You?

What am I to you?
Do I cause the greatest pain,
Or cast a shadow on your name?
Am I a labyrinth to your love,
A barrier to your trust?

Or do I brighten up your day?
Give the essence of vanilla and sage.
Do I ignite your blazing heart?
Rule like the Napoleon Bonaparte.

Well dear love,
I guess I'll never know,
What my characteristics bring to your soul.
For you treat me like some dirt on your shoe,
The sheer neglect has only become accrue.

Oh never mind,
It's how life is destined to be.
If only at first my eyes could see,
Not to hold someone you just cannot rely on,
Or as the Romans would say,
Te futueo et caballum tuum.[1]

---

[1]Futueo you and your horse.

Keira Forde

My Descriptive Thoughts

Bombora

Life moves on
Like the undulation of the ocean.
Don't hang around
Or you'll be swept away by the motion.

Ephemeral

He was perfect
In the way that a plaster
Is perfect.
I was temporarily healed
But I dreaded the day where he'd be torn
Away from me.

Excess

She was the grease to his
Squeaking wheel
But she poured too much
And now he's slipping down the hill.

Loyalty

I would.
After every droplet of torture that
You've poured on my skin
I'd still fall back in your arms.
I would.

———————————————————————

Unavailing

I'm a candle without the opal flame,
A book with no meaningful name.

I'm a willow tree without the signature branches,
A choreographer without good dances.

I've never held myself,
To anything worth pride.
Nothing I would want,
Painted out in the sky.

The most beautiful being,
Who could ever walk this earth,
Is a person who is willing,
To have half of what they wanted at first.

The Garden Of Eden

I am the seedling
to the poisonous fruit tree.
It looks so vibrant and oh so beautiful,
but take a bite and there you'll realise
that the outside was just a way to
tranquilize.
So you won't see the terrible truth,
lying before your ignorant eyes.

MARIAM MANSARAY

Lachrymose

Lachrymose afflicts the heart
Tearing it apart
Harbinger of sorrow
Promising no tomorrow

Instrument of all our woes
Conqueror of young and old
Like a siren I hear it call
Like a sailor I hasten to fall

Free me I beseech thee
Hear me I call to thee
Bring me forth a saviour so
Leave me not a broken soul

Milky Way

Oh tell me the secrets you hide
For I long to be encompassed by it
What beauty you bring to mind
Breathtakingly stealing my wit

Stars as bright as the chariot of Apollo
Tales of celestial splendour silently told
Compelling mortals to sleepily follow
A dancing star I wish to hold

Billions of miles apart we might be
An extinguished light they say you are
But a kindred soul you are to me
Oh show me what lies yonder

My eyes hunger to look upon thee
For you are the Eurydice to my Orpheus
I pray to one day behold thee
And let my heart soar from here to Olympus

Family Tree

Oh mother, my conscience
An epitome of all that is good
A shield formed with unconditional love
Protector of her young against the raging sea of
confusion
A champion of compassion
A Penelope of true character

Oh father, my protector
A sailor against the harsh tide of responsibilities
Keeper of the peace and sanity
An Odysseus of his time
Standing tall against the odds of despair
Shielding us from the unorthodox ways of this
generation
Conquering the herculean task of fatherhood

Oh sister, my confidant
Keeper of secrets and dreams
A shoulder to cry and lean on
A bond transcending even blood and ancestry
Always there to give warm hugs and support
Fighting for others when their strength fails them
Warrior of the weak liken to that of the heroes of old

Oh brother, my keeper
Devoted to his family
Lending a helping hand and a firm one where it is due
Pledging love and loyalty to family and its values
We stand together firmly united
Forever echoing our family motto
"Always and forever "

Love

Love my old nemesis, how fare thee
Unfettered have you come to wreak havoc on my
 heart?
Giving me a false sense of harmony only briefly
Like the fool I am I fall hopelessly
I never seem to learn
Shame on me then
Love you sweet talker
Whispering sweet nothings in my ear
Like a façade I fail to see your real agenda
Clouding my vision like that of a mist
Plotting my downfall with a sinister twist
Heartbroken you leave me with a promise to come
 again
Love you foul gamer
Why must you always leave my heart out of sync
 with my mind?
A grand master of illusion you must be
My deceived heart begs for your devotion
But my mind carries no such notion
It sees my downfall before my heart, for in this game
 of lies it knows all
Love, will thou not answer?
My heart though broken deserves a witty comeback
Father told me not to plead
Mother said take heed
For in this game of chance there can only be one
 champion
My heart sparked a glimmer of hope, but my mind
 already laid the battle plans
Love, you heart monger

Have ye not enough hearts to build your dungeon of
  pain
Or do you still need the heart of this hopeless
  romantic
Who twisted you into hate, into an anti-romantic?
For there is a saying, hurt people do hurt people
Oh well, I guess I am another Greek tragedy
Love, you old soul
Spinning your web of lies
Corrupting the souls of innocents
Bringing with you your army of no-cents
An unending war with different trends in every
  generation
"Till infinity and beyond" they holler

The Patriot

I am a patriot.
You hear them with their baseless accusations and
    arguments,
what do you mean by patriot?
What does it even mean?
How do you know you are a patriot,
and why should I be a patriot to a country that has done
    me nothing but harm?

Is it the country's fault or its ambassadors?
For I have never seen a country in existence without its
    people.
You hear them ask what has my country done for me,
my dear brother and sister, what have you done for your
    country?
You pledged your love and loyalty to your country
    promising to defend her,
but here you are sucking her dry.

I am a patriot.
You see them spending the dues of the people or I dare I
    say the country,
but still with the impetus to call themselves patriot.
My dear I have money to spend, you hear the patriot
    say,
money from the coffers of one's nation that belongs to
    the masses.

You vowed to serve her faithfully but here you are
cheating on her and "borrowing" from her coffers.
Oh my how the word patriot has changed.

I am a patriot.
You hear them bellow, but you see them oppressing the
   people they swore to protect.
Hugging power like a greedy spoilt child,
ignoring the clamour for justice, the outcry of the
   disadvantaged.
Oh mother (country) how we love you, they belch while
"borrowing" mercilessly from the poor.
Ignoring the cries of mother (country) who is
heartbroken from the disunity,
besmirching mother's honour and good name that they
pledged to uphold.

I am a patriot.
You hear them say during elections when it is time to
   campaign, dare I say lie to the people.
And like a battered wife, they believe their oppressors,
and fall back into old habits, continuing the endless loop
   of abuse.
Oh my children, they hear mother (country) cry but as
usual ignore her for the sweet nothings from their
   deceiver.

A country of the deaf or people who perfected
   selective hearing.
Oh my children have ye learnt nothing? Mother
   (cries) with lost hope.

The Scarred Ones

We are the scarred ones
The voice of the helpless
Our souls tormented by our transgressors
They swore to protect us from the world
But they fail to protect us from the monsters within
    them
Our spirits are that of the disadvantaged
Clamouring for justice
Hearts that bleed from the injustice suffered
Some scars are seen and some scars are hidden
Our eyes depict the sorrow within us
Our smile, a façade
Easy to miss by the myopic and lucky ones
We identify ourselves in solidarity by the look in our
    eyes
Nightmares in endless loop of the same abuse
Nowhere to escape without being reminded of our
    trauma
The mirror becomes an enemy,
Because we wrestle with the reflection of the would
    have been happy child
Something that became unattainable the moment we
    became tainted
The would have been happy child smiles at us with
    hopeful eyes
We hate that, we hate smiling and having false sense of
    hope, euphoria
We banish the would have been happy child into the
    deepest darkest part of our mind
We call it the underground
So we can have a conversation with the scarred
    sorrowful child

We wonder if life would have been different if we've
    never been scarred
We quickly banish such thoughts, because they lead us
    into thinking there is hope of escaping being a victim
We know better
If there was a hope of escape, would we want to?
Some would readily accept it
Whiles some of us would think it a trap
Or because the pain is familiar and we do not want to let
    go
Letting go would mean letting go of our anger, fear,
    helplessness, nightmares, disappointment and being a
    victim
Letting go would mean we could be the would have
    been happy child
Letting go would mean we would have nothing to hold
    on to
It would mean we'd have to trust again
It would mean we'd have to heal and be whole again
It all seems like a whole other state of being to us
A new territory uncharted
Maybe we are comforted by a sense of dysphoria
Excuse the pity party
For we are the scarred ones.

Human

Hate as dark as the abyss comes easy to me
So does love as unconditional as a mother's
For these two, no matter how contrary intertwine with
  our being
A dance of destiny likened to that of Ra and Apophis
"What a contradiction you pose to be" they say
My choice is limited, for I am only human

Happiness, though wondrous like that of a new day,
  scares me
The joy it brings makes one as light as a feather
There is always a price to pay for such light
That is why I walk the lane of indifference, neither
  happy nor sad
"My dear, what a sad life you live"
What can I do but say I am only human

Hope is bright and colourful like the wings of Isis
Euphoric bliss enjoyed by optimist making them
  myopic
A pessimist suffers no such shortcomings
For they always expect the unexpected by limiting
  their expectations
For human beings are neither ubiquitous nor
  transcendent
For we are only human

Man they say is free from constraints
But there is only mocked freedom as presented by
  society
For man is born free, and everywhere he is in chains

Death I believe is the breaker of chains that releases
  the soul
"Such a glum view you portray"
Do not blame me for my view for I am only human

Promises made by mortals are as flippant as the mind
  of a child
Hardly ever adhered to by the weak minded
They are inconsistent like the gods of old, ever
  changing
"I will be there to save you" they say
Forgive me for not believing in your promise to save
me
For you are only human and I am as human as I'll
ever

By The River I Wept

By the river I stood and wept
Tear droplets flowing in unison with the river
Creating my own river base
Heart overflowing with dysphoria
Naiads asking why so sorrowful
Mouth so full it cannot speak
A tale of woe told by sad eyes
For lachrymose engulfs this soul
So I wept by a river as cold as the waters of Cocytus
The frozen lake of hell
A question echoed in my soul, why did I come here to
cry and why are my tears falling so fast?
I've lost my way, my sense of being
I can't seem to find it
I wander aimlessly
I lack the patience required
For the path is guarded and narrow
And so, I ended up at the river and I wept to my
heart's content
And they ask, is this your tale of woe?
Yes, this is my tale of woe
You would be woeful too if you lost your way
For I have lost mine

Brown Eyed Boy

They say the eyes are the windows to the soul
For I am the beholder and your eyes have me
  beholden
Iridescent aura with eyes lined with kohl
Bringing to mind your mocha coloured goodness and
  iris so golden
As dark as chocolate, as beautiful as Adonis

Your eyes create a whole new dimension
Hypnotising your beholders
Blessed with dimples and a beautiful smile releasing
  one's tension
Bringing my mind to a place of Zen
An addiction personified

Dark brown eyes and skin resonating with the rich
  African soil
Blessed with the sweet scent of mother nature
Wondering how many you have left in a state of
  turmoil
For you are my brown eyed boy

To Thine Own Self Be True

I am a woman of this generation
A generation known for its misconceptions
Before a step is taken, a voice echoes in my head
'To thine own self be true'
'To thine own self be faithful'
I wrestle with this notion, being a woman of this
generation
I use this notion as a chant, becoming a mantra
'To thine own self be true'
'To thine own self be faithful'
Mantra used as a guiding inspiration
Resonating this with the woman in the mirror
She sometimes adheres to it but other times comes
into conflict with it
For I am human, as human as I'll ever be
But what remains constant as night and day in my
head is
'To thine own self be true'
'To thine own self be faithful'

I Met A Man

I met a man
Eyes depicting the flaws of human nature
I saw the light leave his eyes
Coupled with regret and hopelessness
His eyes met mine and I saw vulnerability
Eyes awaking consciousness
Consciousness seeking heart
My heart weeping for a man I have never met or knew
His being defying death's hold
Convulsing till his last breath
I asked if the man was guilty of the crime
None answered but shrugged forlornly
Why should he be punished without trial?
Guilty or not
Why should one man be judge jury and executioner?
I knew not of his innocence, nor his guilt
For I met a man
Soul tormented by his eyes, they haunt me
Eyes depicting the human condition
A condition we try to hide
I looked at him sorrowfully, unable to help
I try to be myopic again, but I failed
For I met a man and his eyes gave me back my vision

Boy I Have Never Met

Dear boy I have never met
I wish to meet you someday
To tell you how long and far I've searched for you in
   the eyes of strangers
How hard I've been hurt in hope of meeting you
   someday
Sleepless nights filled with longing cries from the
   mishaps of failed attractions
Feelings of regret coupled with sadness at the thought
   of losing someone you've never met
Dreamful slumber of all the good times we never had
In those dreams I'm the girl you wanted and you've
   searched far and wide just to meet me
And for once I was the one that was being searched for
For once I was the one being loved to fruition
A contented heart in a dreamy facade
And then I wake up and feel the emptiness my dreams
   left
The big shoes that my reality cannot fill
Searching for someone you've never met in the arms
   and gaze of utter strangers
They put on masks and pretend to be you
For a while I'm fooled by said mask but I'm eventually
   woken by the stabs of pain
I still search and do the same mistake over and over
   again
Because my sad lovesick heart never learn
What a tragedy my life is turning out to be

A series of unfortunate events longing for a destined
  stranger
I bet when you eventually find me, you will laugh at
  my crazy adventures to find you
This is me hopefully thinking you'll laugh and not run
  away saying such a hopeless loser
I'm hopefully wishing you think of me as the prettiest
  of them all
Because all I have are my hopes and wishes
For someone I'll probably never meet, my heart sure
  do know you

For Love To Be True

Love I believe is a nectar that feeds the soul
Emotions so true that it surpasses Aphrodite's own
Feelings that are not a slave to Cupid's bow
Like the stories of old
Rivalling that of Odysseus and Penelope or that of
Tristan and Isolde.

For love to be true,
Our souls must be bound by its unfettered embrace
Binding us till infinity and beyond
Like the two lovers from Pompeii,
Their love surpassing fear of death
For our love does not discriminate
Its knows neither race nor age
For it is ubiquitous and eternal
Forever echoing our tale like the heroes of old

Simple Things

I long for the simple things
Feeling the wind as it kisses my cheeks
My Hijab billowing in it like a flag
Whispering thousand secrets across the ocean
Hypnotised by the dancing leaves, their grace
For a moment I am one with the wind
Letting it guide me seamlessly to those beautiful secrets
For a moment the universe doesn't seem so vast and I
    feel the connection, the magnetic pull
And in that moment I bow to my Rabb (Lord) and
    praise him for such splendour

The night sky brings with it its own joy
It tells a story with every star in it
A star tells me that it has travelled far, through the
    cosmos to be there in its extinguished state
Some see it as a luminous dot in a cloudless sky
The full moon shines on, putting me in a trance
And I wonder what the heavens would be like
And as I lay under the starry sky, I dream that I'll be
    there one day, near my Rabb

I crave the rays of the sun on my Melanin skin
The warmth it brings to a depressed soul
Sustaining us and giving us solace in dark times
They say joy comes in the morning, but I believe the
    sun brings it
I stand still to hear it whisper its secrets
It tells me that it came from my Rabb
To nourish us and give us the strength to endure

The End

A Literary Portfolio

Books published by Winston:

Air Force Cadet
The Runaway
Airborne Soldiers
The Story of Mining in Sierra Leone
From Aden to Bliss
Reflections on our Independence
Layila Kakatua wan bi Lida

Books Edited by Winston Forde:

Milo and all that Jazz by *Kitty Fadlu Deen*
From Land of Diamonds To The Isle Of Spice by *Sigismond Henry Tucker*
The Incredible History of My Liberated Ancestors by *Charles Harding*
Reflections on My Life by *Arnold Awoonor- Gordon*
Violent Hands:Youths and Murder in 1945 Britain by *Conrad Lisk*
Foulah Tong 1960 and Beyond by *Mohammed Liadi Cole*
Adjai - Bishop Adjai Crowther by *Arnold Awoonor- Gordon*
Blow Out You Bugles by *Conrad Lisk*
My World of Stories by *Esther Shodeke*
Until The Sky Turns Silver by *Diana Skelton and Jean Stallings*
The Golden Gloves of Heracles & Hercules's by *Jermaine Nnamdi Carew*
At a glance by *Keira Forde*
Pains of a Mother by *Hassan Baraka*
Tiger Fist by *Jermaine Nnamdi Carew*

Note: All Books available worldwide on Amazon Books.

www.ingramcontent.com/pod-product-compliance
Lightning Source LLC
Chambersburg PA
CBHW032030251025
34508CB00113B/2146